QUIZ LISTS
QUIZZES

First published in 2002 by Miles Kelly Publishing Ltd,
Bardfield Centre, Great Bardfield, Essex, CM7 4SL

Copyright © Miles Kelly Publishing Ltd 2002

This edition printed 2002

ISBN 1-84236-134-1

2 4 6 8 10 9 7 5 3

Project Manager: Ian Paulyn
Assistant: Lisa Clayden
Design: Clare Sleven

Contact us by email: info@mileskelly.net
Website: www.mileskelly.net

Printed in India

QUIZ LISTS QUIZZES

by
Christopher Rigby

Miles Kelly
PUBLISHING

About the Author

Born in Blackburn, Lancashire in 1960, Christopher Rigby has been compiling and presenting pub quizzes for the past 15 years. When he is not adding to his material for quizzes, Christopher works in the car industry. He is married to Clare – they have two teenage daughters, Hollie and Ashley and share their home with two demented dogs called Vespa and Bailey. A keen Manchester United fan Christopher lists his heroes as George Best and Homer Simpson.

QUIZ LISTS EXPLAINED

The following quiz book contains 90 quizzes of 10 quick fire questions, each group of 10 concentrating on a single theme.

Below is an example:

TITLE ROLES

NAME THE ACTORS WHO PLAYED THE TITLE ROLES IN...

1. *Kojak* (Telly Savalas)
2. *A Touch of Frost* (David Jason)
3. *Frasier* (Kelsey Grammar)
4. *Inspector Morse* (John Thaw)
5. *Shelley* (Hywel Bennett)
6. *Quincy* (Jack Klugman)
7. *Lovejoy* (Ian McShane)
8. *Worzel Gummidge* (Jon Pertwee)
9. *Taggart* (Mark McManus)
10. *Dixon of Dock Green* (Jack Warner)

SESSION 1

SHIP-SHAPE

NAME THE FAMOUS SAILING VESSEL OF THE FOLLOWING TRAVELLERS.

1. Christopher Columbus

2. Jacques Cousteau

3. Popeye

4. Horatio Nelson

5. Blackbeard

6. Captain James Cook

7. Captain Pugwash

8. Pilgrim Fathers

9. Charles Darwin

10. Pinky and Perky

ANSWERS

1. *Santa Maria* 2. *Calypso* 3. *The Olive* 4. HMS *Victory* 5. *Queen Anne's Revenge* 6. *Endeavour* 7. *The Black Pig* 8. *The Mayflower* 9. HMS *Beagle* 10. SS *Melody Maker*

6

FILM CONNECTIONS

NAME THE FILM STAR WHO CONNECTS EACH GROUP OF THREE FILMS.

1. *The Mask*, *The Cable Guy* and *Dumb and Dumber*

2. *Houdini*, *The Great Race* and *The Boston Strangler*

3. *Seven*, *Meet Joe Black* and *Thelma and Louise*

4. *Flatliners*, *Hook* and *The Pelican Brief*

5. *Mermaids*, *Moonstruck* and *Tea With Mussolini*

6. *The Dirty Dozen*, *Cat Ballou* and *Gorky Park*

7. *Little Women*, *Edward Scissorhands* and *Beetlejuice*

8. *Klute*, *The China Syndrome* and *Coming Home*

9. *Speed*, *Chain Reaction* and *Dracula*

10. *All About Eve*, *The Little Foxes* and *Whatever Happened To Baby Jane*

ANSWERS

1. Jim Carrey 2. Tony Curtis 3. Brad Pitt 4. Julia Roberts 5. Cher 6. Lee Marvin 7. Winona Ryder 8. Jane Fonda 9. Keanu Reeves 10. Bette Davis

POETRY IN MOTION

WHO WROTE THE FOLLOWING POEMS?

1. 'The Soldier'

2. 'The Owl And The Pussycat'

3. 'Hiawatha'

4. 'Paradise Lost'

5. 'Kubla Khan'

6. 'Gunga Din'

7. 'Don Juan'

8. 'Twas The Night Before Christmas'

9. 'The Iliad'

10. 'The Charge Of The Light Brigade'

ANSWERS

1. Rupert Brooke 2. Edward Lear 3. Henry Longfellow 4. John Milton 5. Samuel Taylor Coleridge 6. Rudyard Kipling 7. Lord Byron 8. Clement Moore 9. Homer 10. Alfred Tennyson

TV SPIN-OFFS

WHICH TV PROGRAMMES SPAWNED THE FOLLOWING SPIN-OFFS?

1. *Knot's Landing*

2. *Frasier*

3. *Trapper John*

4. *Benson*

5. *The Colbys*

6. *Laverne and Shirley*

7. *George and Mildred*

8. *Tucker's Luck*

9. *The Avengers*

10. *Softly, Softly*

ANSWERS
1. Dallas 2. Cheers 3. MASH 4. Soap 5. Dynasty 6. Happy Days 7. Man About The House
8. Grange Hill 9. Police Surgeon 10. Z Cars

A MUSICAL MENAGERIE

NAME THE NO. I HITS OF THE FOLLOWING RECORDING ARTISTS, ALL OF WHICH CONTAIN A TYPE OF CREATURE IN THE TITLE OF THE SONG.

1. 1982 – Survivor

2. 1978 – Boomtown Rats

3. 1972 – Donny Osmond

4. 1983 – Culture Club

5. 1990 – Partners In Kryme

6. 1982 – Tight Fit

7. 1960 – Johnny Preston

8. 1978 – Brian & Michael

9. 1966 – Manfred Mann

10. 1953 – Lita Roza

ANSWERS

1.'Eye Of The Tiger'. 2.'Rat Trap'. 3.'Puppy Love'. 4.'Karma Chameleon'. 5.'Turtle Power'. 6.'The Lion Sleeps Tonight'. 7.'Running Bear'. 8.'Matchstick Men & Matchstick Cats and Dogs'. 9.'Pretty Flamingo'. 10.'How Much Is That Doggie In The Window?'

CAPITAL B's

NAME THE CAPITAL CITIES, ALL OF WHICH BEGIN WITH THE LETTER B, OF THE FOLLOWING COUNTRIES.

1. Belgium

2. Colombia

3. China

4. Switzerland

5. Lebanon

6. Barbados

7. Hungary

8. Belize

9. Argentina

10. Mali

ANSWERS

1. Brussels 2. Bogota 3. Beijing 4. Berne 5. Beirut 6. Bridgetown 7. Budapest 8. Belmopan 9. Buenos Aires 10. Bamako

SPORTING TERMS

....

IN WHICH SPORT WOULD YOU ...

1. Perform a Rudolph and a Randolph?

2. Throw stones at houses?

3. Use a mashie or a niblick?

4. Stand at silly point?

5. Start at the south stake?

6. Sit in a sulky?

7. Employ the O'Brien shift?

8. Win the Sam McGuire Trophy?

9. Abide by the Cartwright Rules?

10. Trim your sheets?

ANSWERS

1. Trampolining 2. Curling 3. Golf 4. Cricket 5. Croquet 6. Harness-racing 7. Shot putt 8. Gaelic football 9. Baseball 10. Yachting

NATIONAL NUANCES

WHAT IS THE NATIONAL . . .

1. Drink of Russia?

2. Animal of Canada?

3. Flag of France?

4. Flower of Germany?

5. Sport of Bulgaria?

6. Symbol of South Africa?

7. Currency of Korea?

8. Cheese of Greece?

9. Airline of Holland?

10. Anthem of Wales?

ANSWERS

1. Vodka 2. Beaver 3. Tricolour 4. Cornflower 5. Weight-lifting 6. Springbok 7. Won
8. Feta 9. KLM 10. 'Land Of My Fathers'

NUMERICAL NOVELS

....

WHO WROTE THE FOLLOWING NOVELS WITH NUMBERS IN THEIR TITLES?

1. *The Three Musketeers*

2. *1984*

3. *The Thirty-Nine Steps*

4. *The Moon and Sixpence*

5. *A Tale Of Two Cities*

6. *Three Men In A Boat*

7. *The Sign Of Four*

8. *101 Dalmatians*

9. *Anna Of The Five Towns*

10. *20,000 Leagues Under The Sea*

ANSWERS

1. Alexandre Dumas 2. George Orwell 3. John Buchan 4. Somerset Maugham
5. Charles Dickens 6. Jerome K Jerome 7. Arthur Conan Doyle 8. Dodie Smith
9. Arnold Bennett 10. Jules Verne

A BEAST OF A NICKNAME

WHAT ARE THE 'BEASTLY' NICKNAMES OF THE FOLLOWING FIGURES?

1. Greg Norman

2. Anne of Cleves

3. Rommel

4. Rocky Balboa

5. King Richard I

6. Australia's Rugby Union Team

7. Eddie Edwards

8. Derby County FC

9. Ilich Ramirez Sanchez

10. Mansfield Town FC

ANSWERS
1. The Great White Shark 2. The Flanders Mare 3. The Desert Fox 4. The Italian Stallion
5. The Lionheart 6. The Wallabies 7. The Eagle 8. The Rams 9. Carlos the Jackal
10. The Stags

DOWN BY THE RIVERSIDE

....

ON WHICH RIVERS DO THE FOLLOWING CITIES STAND?

1. Vienna

2. Turin

3. Baghdad

4. Paris

5. Pisa

6. New Orleans

7. Cork

8. Calcutta

9. Northampton

10. Madrid

ANSWERS
1. Danube 2. Po 3. Tigris 4. Seine 5. Arno 6. Mississippi 7. Lee 8. Hooghly 9. Nene 10. Manzanares

MONKEY BUSINESS

....

WHAT IS THE NAME OF THE MONKEY ...

1. In the film *Every Which Way But Loose?*

2. That raised Tarzan in the novel?

3. In the film *The Jungle Book?*

4. That are native to Gibraltar?

5. That lived on Skull Island?

6. That gives its name to a blood group?

7. Played by Roddy McDowell in the film The *Planet of the Apes?*

8. In the children's TV show *Pipkins?*

9. In the film *The Lion King?*

10. Who was Ronald Reagan's co-star in several films?

ANSWERS

1. Clyde 2. Kala 3. King Louie 4. Barbary Apes 5. King Kong 6. Rhesus 7. Cornelius 8. Topov 9. Rafiki 10. Bonzo

TRIBUTE TUNES

....

NAME THE SONG THAT ...

1. Chris De Burgh sang about his wife.

2. Roberta Flack sang about Don McLean.

3. John Denver sang about his wife.

4. Eric Clapton sang about Patti Boyd.

5. Elkie Brooks sang about Janis Joplin.

6. Don McLean sang about the painter of *Irises*

7. Mike Oldfield wrote about John Lennon.

8. Stevie Wonder sang about Martin Luther King.

9. Phil Lynott wrote for his daughter.

10. Elton John sang about Billie Jean King.

ANSWERS

1. 'Lady In Red', 2. 'Killing Me Softly With His Song', 3. 'Annie's Song', 4. 'Layla', 5. 'Pearl's A Singer', 6. 'Vincent' 7. 'Moonlight Shadow', 8. 'Happy Birthday', 9. 'Sarah', 10. 'Philadelphia Freedom'.

18

COLLECTIVELY SPEAKING

IF A PRIDE OF L = LIONS, WHAT DO THE FOLLOWING = ?

1. A murder of C

2. A drove of P

3. A school of W

4. A cast of H

5. An army of F

6. A troop of M

7. A brood of C

8. A skulk of F

9. A cete of B

10. A knot of T

ANSWERS
1. Crows 2. Pigs 3. Whales 4. Hawks 5. Frogs 6. Monkeys 7. Chickens 8. Foxes 9. Badgers 10. Toads

NAME THE NATION

....

IN WHICH COUNTRIES ARE THE FOLLOWING CITIES?

1. Haarlem

2. Casablanca

3. Basra

4. Bilbao

5. Mercedes

6. Guadalajara

7. Odense

8. Innsbruck

9. Monrovia

10. Phnom Penh

KID'S STUFF

IN WHICH CHILDREN'S TV PROGRAMMES DO THE FOLLOWING APPEAR?

1. Tobermory

2. Officer Dibble

3. Penfold

4. Zelda

5. Barney Gumble

6. Pigs in Space

7. Miss Kiki Frog

8. The Iron Chicken

9. Witchiepoo

10. A talking cat called Salem

ANSWERS
1. The Wombles 2. Top Cat 3. Dangermouse 4. Terrahawks 5. The Simpsons 6. The Muppet Show 7. Hector's House 8. The Clangers 9. H R Pufnstuf 10. Sabrina The Teenage Witch

COMMERCIAL BREAK

WHAT PRODUCTS ARE ADVERTISED BY THE FOLLOWING SLOGANS?

1. The lion goes from strength to strength

2. Make teabags make tea.

3. Probably the best lager in the world.

4. The patron saint of pipe smokers

5. Sweets with the less fattening centre

6. Bakers born and bred

7. The ring of confidence

8. Made in Scotland from girders

9. Makes exceedingly good cakes

10 The trouble is they taste too good

ANSWERS
1. Peugeot 2. Tetley 3. Carlsberg 4. St Bruno 5. Maltesers 6. Warburtons 7. Colgate 8. Irn Bru 9. Mr Kipling 10. Kellogg's Crunchy Nut Cornflakes

THINK OF A NUMBER

HOW MANY ...

1. Holes in a ten-pin bowling ball?

2. Legs on a shrimp?

3. Hulls on a catamaran?

4. Pennies in a pre-decimal pound?

5. Keys on a piano?

6. Labours performed by Hercules?

7. Inches in a cubit?

8. Shillings in a guinea?

9. Numbers on a bingo board?

10. States in the USA beginning with M?

ANSWERS

1. 3 2. 10 3. 2 4. 240 5. 88 6. 12 7. 18 8. 21 9. 90 10. 8 – Maine, Maryland, Michigan, Massachusetts, Minnesota, Montana, Missouri and Mississippi

COMEDY CHARACTERS

IN WHICH TV SITCOM DID ...

1. Danny de Vito play Louie De Palma?

2. Michael J Fox play Michael Flaherty?

3. Stephen Lewis play Inspector Blake?

4. George Layton play Bombardier Solomons?

5. Gary Coleman play Arnold Jackson?

6. Matthew Perry play Chandler Bing?

7. Alexei Sayle play Mr Balowski?

8. George Wendt play Norm Petersen?

9. Leslie Nielsen play Detective Frank Drebin?

10. Peter Vaughan play Harry Grout?

ANSWERS

1. Taxi 2. Spin City 3. On the Buses 4. It Ain't Half Hot Mum 5. Different Strokes 6. Friends 7. The Young Ones 8. Cheers 9. Police Squad 10. Porridge

MARKS OUT OF TEN

....

NAME THE MARK WHO ...

1. Wrote *The Prince and The Pauper*.

2. Fronts Dire Straits.

3. Shot John Lennon.

4. Played Luke Skywalker.

5. Sang 'Clementine' and 'Child'.

6. Played Joe Mangle in *Neighbours*.

7. Duetted with Gene Pitney on the song 'Something's Gotten Hold Of My Heart'.

8. Presents *Never Mind The Buzzcocks*.

9. Fell in love with Cleopatra.

10. Died in a car crash, September 16th 1977.

HUSBANDS AND WIVES

....

NAME THE MARRIED COUPLES WHO CO-STARRED IN THE FOLLOWING FILMS AND TV PROGRAMMES.

1. *Fawlty Towers*

2. *Who's Afraid of Virginia Woolf?*

3. *Eyes Wide Shut*

4. *I Love Lucy*

5. *Traffic*

6. *The Drowning Pool*

7. *A Fine Romance*

8. *Forever Green*

9. *The Getaway 1972*

10. *The Getaway 1994*

ANSWERS

1. John Cleese and Connie Booth 2. Richard Burton and Liz Taylor 3. Tom Cruise and Nicole Kidman 4. Desi Arnez and Lucille Ball 5. Michael Douglas and Catherine Zeta Jones 6. Paul Newman and Joanne Woodward 7. Michael Williams and Judi Dench 8. John Alderton and Pauline Collins 9. Steve McQueen and Ali McGraw 10. Alec Baldwin and Kim Basinger

WORLD CITY SIGHTS

IN WHICH WORLD CITIES WOULD YOU FIND THE FOLLOWING FAMOUS SIGHTS?

1. The Golden Gate Bridge

2. The Raffles Western Hotel

3. The Wailing Wall

4. Sears Tower

5. The Mannekin Pis

6. The Petronas Tower

7. The Church of St Basil

8. The World Trade Center

9. The Golden Temple

10. The Alhambra Palace

ANSWERS
1. San Francisco 2. Singapore 3. Jerusalem 4. Chicago 5. Brussels 6. Kuala Lumpar
7. Moscow 8. New York 9. Amritsar 10. Granada

ENGLISH CITY SIGHTS

....

IN WHICH ENGLISH CITY WOULD YOU FIND THE FOLLOWING?

1. The Crucible Theatre

2. Clifton Suspension Bridge

3. Crosby Airport

4. The National Watersports Centre

5. The Tamar Bridge

6. The University of East Anglia

7. The National Exhibition Centre

8. The National Railway Museum

9. The Royal Seaforth Docks

10. The Mayflower Memorial

ANSWERS
1. Sheffield 2. Bristol 3. Carlisle 4. Nottingham 5. Plymouth 6. Norwich 7. Birmingham 8. York 9. Liverpool 10. Southampton

SINGING SOAP STARS

NAME THE SOAP STARS WHO HAD HITS WITH THE FOLLOWING.

1. 'Anyone Can Fall In Love'

2. 'Torn'

3. 'Every Loser Wins'

4. 'I Should Be So Lucky'

5. 'Happy Just To Be With You'

6. 'Hillbilly Rock, Hillbilly Roll'

7. 'Any Dream Will Do'

8. 'Sunburn'

9. 'Mona'

10. 'Don't Pull Your Love'

ANSWERS

1. Anita Dobson 2. Natalie Imbruglia 3. Nick Berry 4. Kylie Minogue 5. Michelle Gayle 6. The Woolpackers 7. Jason Donovan 8. Michelle Collins 9. Craig McLachlan 10. Sean McGuire

NOVEL LOCATIONS

**NAME THE FAMOUS NOVELS THAT WERE
SET HERE.**

1. Lilliput

2. Airstrip One

3. St Petersburg

4. Ruritania

5. The Catskill Mountains

6. The Celestial City

7. Dingley Dell

8. Middle Earth

9. Narnia

10. Prince Edward Island

BODY MATTERS

....

IN THE HUMAN BODY WHAT IS THE MORE COMMON NAME FOR THESE ANATOMICAL TERMS?

1. The cranium

2. The lacrymal glands

3. The uterus

4. The larynx

5. The scapula

6. Third molars

7. The trachea

8. The axilla

9. Sebhorric dermatitis

10. The hallux

ANSWERS
1. Skull 2. Tear ducts 3. Womb 4. Adam's apple 5. Shoulder blade 6. Wisdom teeth 7. Windpipe 8. Armpit 9. Dandruff 10. Big toe

PHONETICALLY SPEAKING

....

IN THE PHONETIC ALPHABET WHICH
WORDS REPRESENT THE FOLLOWING LETTERS?

1. W

2. L

3. R

4. Q

5. G

6. S

7. V

8. E

9. T

10. F

TV THEMES

WHO PERFORMED THE THEME SONGS FOR THE FOLLOWING TV SERIES?

1. *One Foot In The Grave*

2. *Neighbours*

3. *Dad's Army*

4. *Friends*

5. *The Liver Birds*

6. *Auf Wiedersehen Pet*

7. *The Royle Family*

8. *The Love Boat*

9. *Brush Strokes*

10. *Absolutely Fabulous*

ANSWERS

1. Eric Idle 2. Tony Hatch 3. Bud Flanagan 4. The Rembrandts 5. The Scaffold 6. Joe Fagin 7. Oasis 8. Jack Jones 9. Kevin Rowlands 10. Julie Driscoll, Brian Auger and the Trinity

33

TO BE OR NOT TO BE

....

NAME THE SHAKESPEARE PLAY ...

1. That begins with a storm at sea.

2. That features the murder of King Duncan.

3. That contains the most words.

4. That is sub-titled *The Moor of Venice*.

5. In which Shylock appeared.

6. That has a capital city in its title.

7. That is sub-titled *Or What You Will*.

8. That contains an English place name in its title.

9. That contains the name of an animal in its title.

10. That is set in Vienna.

THE WONDERFUL WORLD OF DISNEY

NAME THE DISNEY ANIMATION THAT FEATURES THE FOLLOWING SONGS.

1. 'When I See An Elephant Fly'

2. 'Circle Of Life'

3. 'Once Upon A Dream'

4. 'Everybody Wants To Be A Cat'

5. 'I Wanna Be Like You'

6. 'A Whole New World'

7. 'Be My Guest'

8. 'Under The Sea'

9. 'Little April Showers'

10. 'Bibbidi-bobbidi-boo'

ANSWERS
1. Dumbo 2. The Lion King 3. Sleeping Beauty 4. The Aristocats 5. The Jungle Book 6. Aladdin 7. Beauty And The Beast 8. The Little Mermaid 9. Bambi 10. Cinderella

CAR TROUBLE

**NAME THE COUNTRIES THAT ARE REPRESENTED
BY THE FOLLOWING INTERNATIONAL
REGISTRATION PLATES.**

1. CY

2. UA

3. D

4. TT

5. H

6. CO

7. MA

8. LV

9. RSM

10. SD

ANSWERS
1. Cyprus 2. Ukraine 3. Germany 4. Trinidad and Tobago 5. Hungary 6. Colombia
7. Morocco 8. Latvia 9. San Marino 10. Swaziland

'S' NOVELISTS

NAME THE AUTHORS OF THE FOLLOWING NOVELS WHO ALL HAVE SURNAMES BEGINNING WITH THE LETTER S.

1. *Ivanhoe*

2. *Frankenstein*

3. *Dracula*

4. *A Town Like Alice*

5. *Blott On The Landscape*

6. *The Grapes Of Wrath*

7. *The Loneliness Of The Long Distance Runner*

8. *The Jewel In The Crown*

9. *Gulliver's Travels*

10. *The Strange Case of Dr Jekyll and Mr Hyde*

ANSWERS

1. Sir Walter Scott 2. Mary Shelley 3. Bram Stoker 4. Neville Shute 5. Tom Sharpe 6. John Steinbeck 7. Alan Sillitoe 8. Paul Scott 9. Jonathan Swift 10. Robert Louis Stevenson

THE STATE OF THINGS

IN WHICH AMERICAN STATE WOULD YOU FIND THE FOLLOWING?

1. Death Valley

2. The Kennedy Space Center

3. Fort Knox

4. The Grand Canyon

5. Las Vegas

6. The Garden of the Gods

7. Mount Rushmore

8. O'Hare Airport

9. Jefferson City

10. Waikiki Beach

ANSWERS
1. California 2. Florida 3. Kentucky 4. Arizona 5. Nevada 6. Colorado 7. South Dakota 8. Illinois 9. Missouri 10. Hawaii

FOOD FOR THOUGHT

NAME THE FOOD STUFFS OR DISHES FROM THE FOLLOWING DESCRIPTIONS.

1. Small cubes of fried or toasted bread.

2. Thick spicy fish soup from Provence

3. Crushed grain, nuts and dried fruit

4. Salted and glazed biscuit shaped like a knot.

5. French for 'flight in the wind'

6. Black German rye bread

7. Indian deep-fried triangular pasty

8. Beef dish named after a 19th-century Russian diplomat

9. Sauce containing mushrooms, shallots, white wine and herbs

10. Thin round Mexican maize cake

ANSWERS
1. Croutons 2. Bouillabaisse 3. Muesli 4. Pretzels 5. Vol-au-vent 6. Pumpernickle 7. Samosa 8. Stroganoff 9. Chasseur 10. Tortilla

CLASSICAL COMPOSERS

....

WHAT NATIONALITY ARE THE FOLLOWING COMPOSERS?

1. Johann Sebastian Bach

2. Georges Bizet

3. Frederic Chopin

4. Frederick Delius

5. Joseph Franz Haydn

6. Giacomo Puccini

7. George Gershwin

8. Antonin Dvorak

9. Sergei Rachmaninov

10. Jean Sibelius

IT'S THE SIZE THAT COUNTS

....

WHAT IS THE ...

1. Largest Canary Island?

2. Largest internal organ?

3. Smallest American state?

4. Highest judo grade?

5. Tallest breed of dog?

6. Largest country in South America?

7. Biggest container port in Britain?

8. Widest river in the world?

9. Highest mountain in Africa?

10. Longest ship canal in the world?

ANSWERS
1. Tenerife 2. Liver 3. Rhode Island 4. 12th Dan 5. Irish wolfhound 6. Brazil
7. Felixstowe 8. Amazon 9. Kilimanjaro 10. St Lawrence Seaway

MOST OF WHAT FOLLOWS IS TRUE

....

NAME THE REAL-LIFE PERSON WHO INSPIRED THE FOLLOWING FILMS.

1. *The Greatest*

2. *What's Love Got To Do With It*

3. *1492*

4. *Rogue Trader*

5. *Great Balls Of Fire*

6. *Lady Sings The Blues*

7. *My Left Foot*

8. *Dance With A Stranger*

9. *The Inn of Sixth Happiness*

10. *Cry Freedom*

MINE HOST

....

WHO COMPERES THE FOLLOWING TV GAME SHOWS?

1. *Tele Addicts*

2. *My Kind Of Music*

3. *15 TO 1*

4. *Countdown*

5. *The Weakest Link*

6. *Don't Forget Your Toothbrush*

7. *They Think It's All Over*

8. *Screen Test*

9. *It's Only TV But I Like It*

10. *Beat The Teacher*

ARTIST ANSWERS

WHO PAINTED THE FOLLOWING MASTERPIECES?

1. *The Haywain*

2. *The Last Supper*

3. *210 Coca Cola Bottles*

4. *Portrait Of Dr Gachet*

5. *Going To The Match*

6. *Guernica*

7. *The Laughing Cavalier*

8. *The Night Watch*

9. The ceiling of the Sistine Chapel

10. *Samson and Delilah*

ANSWERS

1. John Constable 2. Leonardo da Vinci 3. Andy Warhol 4. Vincent Van Gogh 5. L S Lowry 6. Pablo Picasso 7. Franz Hals 8. Rembrandt 9. Michelangelo 10. Peter Paul Rubens

MANS BEST FRIEND

. . . .

NAME THE PET DOGS OF THESE FAMOUS FIGURES.

1. Dennis the Menace

2. Dr Who

3. Punch and Judy

4. Roy Rogers

5. Bart Simpson

6. Bill Sykes

7. Crystal Tipps

8. Dorothy Gale

9. The Waltons

10. The Jetsons

ANSWERS

1. Gnasher 2. K9 3. Toby 4. Bullet 5. Santa's Little Helper 6. Bullseye 7. Alastair 8. Toto 9. Reckless 10. Astro

THE COUNTY SET

IN WHICH ENGLISH COUNTY WOULD YOU FIND THE FOLLOWING?

1. Haworth Parsonage

2. Luton Airport

3. Stonehenge

4. Blenheim Palace

5. The National Football Museum

6. Bodmin Moor

7. Eton College

8. Jodrell Bank

9. Wookey Hole Cave

10. Fotheringay Castle

ANSWERS

1. Yorkshire 2. Bedfordshire 3. Wiltshire 4. Oxfordshire 5. Lancashire 6. Cornwall 7. Berkshire 8. Cheshire 9. Somerset 10. Northamptonshire

IT STARTED WITH AN I!

NAME THE NO. 1 HITS OF THE FOLLOWING ARTISTS,
THE TITLES OF WHICH ALL BEGIN WITH
THE WORD I.

1. 1979 – Boomtown Rats

2. 1962 – Frank Ifield

3. 1984 – Stevie Wonder

4. 1987 – Aretha Franklin & George Michael

5. 1979 – Gloria Gaynor

6. 1969 – Marvin Gaye

7. 1982 – Eddy Grant

8. 1984 – Foreigner

9. 1999 – Backstreet Boys

10. 1997 – Eternal

ANSWERS

1. 'I Don't Like Mondays' 2. 'I Remember You' 3. 'I Just Called To Say I Love You'
4. 'I Knew You Were Waiting' 5. 'I Will Survive' 6. 'I Heard It Through The Grapevine'
7. 'I Don't Wanna Dance' 8. 'I Want To Know What Love Is' 9. 'I Want It That Way'
10. 'I Wanna Be The Only One'

TV ACRONYMS

WHAT DO THE FOLLOWING ACRONYMS STAND FOR?

1. *TISWAS*

2. TARDIS in *Dr Who*

3. *MASH*

4. WIN in *Joe 90*

5. *The Man From UNCLE*

6. *ER*

7. *CATS Eyes*

8. *Danger UXB*

9. *NYPD Blue*

10. WASP in *Stingray*

ANSWERS

1. Today is Saturday Watch and Smile 2. Time and Relative Dimension in Space 3. Mobile Army Surgical Hospital 4. World Intelligence Network 5. United Network Command for Law Enforcement 6. Emergency Room 7. Covert Activities Thames Section 8. Unexploded Bomb 9. New York Police Department 10. World Aquanaut Sea Patrol

FAMILY AFFAIRS

WHAT ARE THE SURNAMES OF THE FOLLOWING FAMILIES FROM THE WORLD OF ENTERTAINMENT?

1. Peter, Jane, Henry and Bridget

2. Beau, Jeff and Lloyd

3. Hayley, Juliet and John

4. Marlon, Tito, Michael, Janet and Jermaine

5. Lionel, Ethel and John

6. William, Alec, Daniel and Stephen

7. John, Julian and Sean

8. Nadim, Nadia and Julia

9. Walter, Angelica and John

10. Linda, Colleen, Maureen and Bernadette

ANSWERS
1. Fonda 2. Bridges 3. Mills 4. Jackson 5. Barrymore 6. Baldwin 7. Lennon 8. Sawalha
9. Huston 10. Nolan

49

NOVEL ANAGRAMS

UNRAVEL THE ANAGRAMS TO GIVE THE TITLE OF A FAMOUS NOVEL.

1. NOODLE ROAN

2. HE BIT BOTH

3. ON A HIVE

4. WASHTIN POWDER

5. SHE SANG A SALE

6. RUB HEN

7. LOW MEN TITLE

8. OFTEN A SEED

9. GRAN RUED BABY

10. SPITTING AT RON

COLOURFUL CAPERS

WHAT COLOUR IS EACH OF THE FOLLOWING?

1. The flag of Libya

2. An amethyst

3. A female blackbird

4. A moonstone

5. The largest mammal in the world

6. Sir Percy Blakeney's pseudonym

7. A Clanger

8. The birthstone for January

9. *Thunderbird 4*

10. The murder victim in Cluedo

ANSWERS
1. Green 2. Violet 3. Brown 4. White 5. Blue Whale 6. Scarlet Pimpernel 7. Pink
8. Red Garnet 9. Yellow 10. Doctor Black

LEADERS OF THE GANG

WHO IS THE LEAD SINGER OF THE FOLLOWING GROUPS?

1. Nirvana

2. Wizzard

3. The Sex Pistols

4. Spandau Ballet

5. Blur

6. The Verve

7. The Human League

8. The Kinks

9. Bad Manners

10. Everything but the Girl

ANSWERS
1. Kurt Cobane 2. Roy Wood 3. Johnny Rotten AKA John Lydon 4. Tony Hadley
5. Damon Albarn 6. Richard Ashcroft 7. Phil Oakey 8. Ray Davies 9. Buster Bloodvessel
10. Tracy Thorn

FAMOUS FIRSTS

....

WHO, WHAT OR WHICH WAS THE FIRST ...

1. Man to play golf on the moon?

2. Name of Mrs Beeton?

3. Decade in which Oscars were awarded?

4. Duo to be inducted into the Rock and Roll Hall of Fame?

5. Captain of the USS *Enterprise*?

6. Country to employ the metric system?

7. Boxer to regain the World Heavyweight title?

8. Film to be made with stereo soundtrack?

9. Woman to present *Grandstand*?

10. No. 1 hit to feature bagpipes?

ANSWERS

1. Alan Shephard 2. Isabella 3. 1920s 4. Everly Brothers 5. Christopher Pike 6. France 7. Floyd Patterson 8. *Fantasia* 9. Helen Rollason 10. 'Amazing Grace'

WHAT'S YOUR POISON

WHAT IS THE FAVOURITE DRINK OF EACH OF THE FOLLOWING CHARACTERS?

1. Arthur Daley

2. Bacchus

3. Mike Baldwin

4. Hopalong Cassidy

5. The Famous Five

6. Ena Sharples

7. James Bond

8. Homer Simpson

9. The Wurzels

10. Worzel Gummidge

M PEOPLE

·····························

ALL THE FOLLOWING ARE THE REAL NAMES OF FAMOUS PEOPLE WHO ARE BETTER KNOWN BY A SURNAME BEGINNING WITH THE LETTER M.

1. Georgios Panayiotou

2. Ludvik Hoch

3. Roberta Joan Anderson

4. Ilynea Mironoff

5. Harold Sargent

6. Barry Pincus

7. Norma Jean Baker

8. Reginald Truscott-Jones

9. Helen Mitchell

10. Walter Williams

ANSWERS
1. George Michael 2. Robert Maxwell 3. Joni Mitchell 4. Helen Mirren 5. Max Miller 6. Barry Manilow 7. Marilyn Monroe 8. Ray Milland 9. Nellie Melba 10. Bill Mynard

FILM THEMES

....

WHO SANG THE THEME SONG FOR THE
FOLLOWING FILMS?

1. *Fame*

2. *Born Free*

3. *To Sir With Love*

4. *Rocky III*

5. *Move Over Darling*

6. *Wild, Wild West*

7. *Grease*

8. *Goldeneye*

9. *Ghostbusters*

10. *Footloose*

LOSERS

WHO LOST ...

1. Her pocket in a nursery rhyme?

2. Billions of pounds causing Baring's Bank to crash?

3. His World Title to James 'Buster' Douglas?

4. His way in the 1982 Paris–Dakar Rally?

5. Her head in 1536 for alleged adultery?

6. Her heart to a starship trooper?

7. His hand in the film *The Vikings*?

8. The 1999 European Cup Final in injury time?

9. The Battle of the Nile?

10. His liberty after faking his suicide in 1973?

ANSWERS

1. Lucy Lockett 2. Nick Leeson 3. Mike Tyson 4. Mark Thatcher 5. Anne Boleyn 6. Sarah Brightman 7. Tony Curtis 8. Bayern Munich 9. France 10. John Stonehouse

CREATURE COLLECTIVES

....

WHAT SORT OF ANIMAL HAS THE FOLLOWING VARIETIES?

1. Humpbacked, killer and sperm

2. Leghorn, Buff Orpington and Plymouth Rocks

3. Khaki Campbell, mallard and muscovy

4. Pipistrelle, vampire and long-eared

5. Tamworth, saddleback and large white

6. Copperhead, mamba and boomslang

7. Weddell, elephant and Ross

8. Raft, house and trapdoor

9. Colorado, death-watch and Goliath

10. Burchell's, mountain and Grevy's

ANSWERS
1. Whale 2. Chicken 3. Duck 4. Bat 5. Pig 6. Snake 7. Seal 8. Spider 9. Beetle
10. Zebra

NAME THE YEAR

IN WHICH YEAR OF THE 20TH CENTURY DID THE FOLLOWING EVENTS TAKE PLACE?

1. Did Winston Churchill die?

2. Was Pearl Harbor bombed by Japanese fighters?

3. Did the Chernobyl disaster occur?

4. Was the first ever National Lottery draw?

5. Was the first F A Cup Final played at Wembley?

6. Was the farthing withdrawn from circulation?

7. Did Alaska become the 49th American state?

8. Did Princess Anne marry Captain Mark Phillips?

9. Did Princess Anne marry Tim Laurence?

10. Did Queen Victoria die?

ANSWERS
1. 1965 2. 1941 3 1986 4. 1994 5. 1923 6. 1960 7. 1959 8. 1973 9. 1992 10. 1901

6

PLACE THE PROGRAMME

IN WHICH AMERICAN TOWNS OR CITIES WERE THE FOLLOWING TV PROGRAMMES SET?

1. *Hill Street Blues*

2. *Cheers*

3. *Cannon*

4. *Hawaii 5–0*

5. *Little House On The Prairie*

6. *The Golden Girls*

7. *Frasier*

8. *Married With Children*

9. *A Man Called Ironside*

10. *Northern Exposure*

WATCHING THE DETECTIVES

NAME THE DETECTIVE THAT ...

1. Lived in the village of St Mary Mead.

2. Was also known as 'The Saint'.

3. Was created by Dorothy L Sayers.

4. Went in search of the Maltese Falcon.

5. Had a brother called Mycroft.

6. Drove a Peugeot 403 cabriolet.

7. First appeared in a novel called *I The Jury*

8. Was played by Angela Lansbury in *Murder She Wrote*.

9. Was created by Edward Stratemeyer.

10. Owned a bloodhound called Pedro.

ANSWERS

1. Miss Marple 2. Simon Templar 3. Lord Peter Wimsey 4. Sam Spade 5. Sherlock Holmes 6. Colombo 7. Mike Hammer 8. Jessica Fletcher 9. Nancy Drew 10. Sexton Blake

TRANSLATION TEASERS

···

WHAT IS THE LITERAL ENGLISH TRANSLATION OF THE FOLLOWING WORDS OR PHRASES?

1. Bambino

2. Blitzkrieg

3. Nova

4. Déjà vu

5. Volvo

6. Sinn Fein

7. Compos mentis

8. Biscuit

9. Fido

10. Esperanto

ANSWERS

1. Baby 2. Lightning war 3. New 4. Already seen 5. I roll 6. Ourselves Alone 7. In right mind 8. Baked twice 9. I trust 10. One who hopes

A QUESTION OF QUOTES

WHO SAID THE FOLLOWING MEMORABLE WORDS?

1. 'A horse, a horse my kingdom for a horse'

2. 'The lady is not for turning'

3. 'Bugger Bogner' (on his deathbed)

4. 'Genius is 99% perspiration, and 1% inspiration'

5. 'Let them eat cake'

6. 'The ballot is stronger than the bullet'

7. 'Dr Livingstone, I presume?'

8. 'Religion is the opium of the people'

9. 'They think it's all over, it is now' (in 1966)

10. 'When I am dead and open'd you shall find Calais lying in my heart'

ANSWERS

1. Richard III 2. Margaret Thatcher 3. King George V 4. Thomas Edison 5. Marie Antoinette 6. Abraham Lincoln 7. Henry Stanley 8. Karl Marx 9. Kenneth Wolstenholme 10. Mary I

LET'S GO FOR A WALK

WHO SANG THE FOLLOWING 'STROLLING' SONGS?

1. 1961 – 'Walkin' Back To Happiness'

2. 1995 – 'Walking In Memphis'

3. 1985 – 'Walking On Sunshine'

4. 1973 – 'Walk On The Wild Side'

5. 1986 – 'Walk This Way'

6. 1967 – 'Walk Away Renee'

7. 1963 – 'You'll Never Walk Alone'

8. 1985 – 'Walking In The Air'

9. 1963 – 'Walk Like A Man'

10. 1980 – 'A Walk In The Park'

ANSWERS

1. Helen Shapiro 2. Cher 3. Katrina and the Waves 4. Lou Reed 5. Run DMC featuring Aerosmith 6. The Four Tops 7. Gerry and the Pacemakers 8. Aled Jones 9. The Four Seasons 10. Nick Straker Band

RHYMING RIDDLES

IN COCKNEY RHYMING SLANG WHAT WORD IS REPRESENTED BY THE FOLLOWING PHRASES?

1. Well hung

2. Cain and Abel

3. China plate

4. Ayrton Senna

5. Buttons and bows

6. Bill stickers

7. Oxo cube

8. Cloud seven

9. Barnet fair

10. West Ham reserves

ANSWERS
1.Young 2.Table 3. Mate 4.Tenner 5.Toes 6. Knickers 7.Tube 8. Heaven 9. Hair
10. Nerves

WHAT COMES NEXT?

WHO OR WHAT COMES NEXT IN THE FOLLOWING LISTS?

1. QWERTY.

2. Wilding, Todd, Fisher

3. Nixon, Ford, Carter, Reagan

4. Edward I, Edward II, Edward III, Richard II

5. Hartnell, Troughton, Pertwee

6. *Silence Of The Lambs, Unforgiven, Schindler's List, Forrest Gump*

7. Dragon, snake, horse, sheep, monkey, chicken, dog, pig

8. *And Now For Something Completely Different, Monty Python And The Holy Grail, The Life Of Brian*

9. Brazil, Brazil, England, Brazil, West Germany

10. Pugh, Pugh, Barney McGrew, Guthbert, Dibble

ANSWERS

1. U – letters on a keyboard 2. Burton – husbands of Liz Taylor 3. Bush – US Presidents 4. Henry IV – Kings of England 5. Baker – Dr Who 6. *Braveheart* – Best Film Oscars in the 90s 7. Rat – Chinese calendar 8. *The Meaning of Life* – Python films 9. Argentina – winners of football's World Cup 10. Grubb – Trumpton firemen

SOAPSUDS

IN WHICH TV SOAP OPERAS DO THE FOLLOWING CHARACTERS APPEAR?

1. Beppe di Marco

2. Harold Bishop

3. Tracy Corkill

4. Sandy Richardson

5. Chase Gioberti

6. Lucille Hewitt

7. Rodney Harrington

8. Chris Tate

9. Donald Fisher

10. Sergio Munoz D'Avila

ANSWERS
1. *EastEnders* 2. *Neighbours* 3. *Brookside* 4. *Crossroads* 5. *Falcon Crest* 6. *Coronation Street* 7. *Peyton Place* 8. *Emmerdale* 9. *Home And Away* 10. *Eldorado*

GOING FOR GOLD

WHICH COUNTRIES DID THE FOLLOWING GOLD-MEDAL-WINNING ATHLETES REPRESENT?

1. Bob Beamon

2. Said Aouita

3. Merlene Ottey

4. Sergey Bubka

5. John Walker

6. Lasse Viren

7. Emil Zatopek

8. Ingrid Kristiansen

9. Joaquim Cruz

10. Alberto Juantorena

ANSWERS
1. USA 2. Morocco 3. Jamaica 4. USSR and CIS 5. New Zealand 6. Finland 7. Czechoslovakia 8. Norway 9. Brazil 10. Cuba

EVERYTHING ENDS WITH A G

THE ANSWERS TO THE FOLLOWING TEN QUICK-FIRE QUESTIONS ALL END WITH THE LETTER G.

1. Capital of China?

2. Stage name of Gordon Sumner?

3. Hitler's favourite film?

4. Ben Grimm's alter ego in The Fantastic Four?

5. Unit of currency in Vietnam?

6. She sang of 'Constant Craving'?

7. He sang 'Stand By Me'?

8. Two sports that take place on the piste?

9. Film featuring the song 'I've Had The Time Of My Life'?

10. Petula Clark hit written by Charlie Chaplin?

ANSWERS

1. Beijing 2. Sting 3. King Kong 4. The Thing 5. Dong 6. kd Lang 7. Ben E King 8. Skiing and fencing 9. *Dirty Dancing* 10. 'This Is My Song'

FILM ANAGRAMS

UNRAVEL THE FOLLOWING ANAGRAMS TO GIVE THE TITLE OF A FAMOUS FILM.

1. THE RAVE BRA

2. THAT MIXER

3. TIGER RUT

4. MARC A CORNY SINGER

5. LOCAL RATTLE

6. WHALE ON PLATE

7. MAYFLY RAID

8. PAN TOOL

9. NEW TRAMP TOY

10. GREET A PEST ACHE

L OF A NOVEL

NAME THE NOVELS BEGINNING WITH THE LETTER L THAT FEATURED THE FOLLOWING CHARACTERS.

1. Oliver Barrett

2. Chingachoock

3. Sauron the Great

4. Jan Valjean

5. Amy, Jo, Meg and Beth

6. Dolores Haze

7. James Dixon

8. Flora Finching

9. Mr Hobbs the grocer

10. Captain Mallison

ANSWERS
1. Love Story 2. Last of the Mohicans 3. Lord Of The Rings 4. Les Miserables 5. Little Women 6. Lolita 7. Lucky Jim 8. Lucky Jim 9. Little Dorrit 10. Lost Horizon

71

CHART DEBUTS

WHAT WAS THE FIRST TOP 20 UK HIT
SINGLE FOR THE FOLLOWING?

1. The Beatles

2. Westlife

3. Queen

4. Elvis Presley

5. Cliff Richard

6. Thin Lizzy

7. Duran Duran

8. Madonna

9. The Carpenters

10. Mariah Carey

SPORT ON THE SCREEN

WHICH SPORT FEATURED IN THE FOLLOWING FILMS?

1. *The Color of Money*

2. *Best Shot*

3. *This Sporting Life*

4. *Tin Cup*

5. *Pharlap*

6. *A League Of Their Own*

7. *The Main Event*

8. *When Saturday Comes*

9. *American Flyers*

10. *California Dolls*

ANSWERS
1. Pool 2. Basketball 3. Rugby League 4. Golf 5. Horse-racing 6. Baseball 7. Boxing 8. Football 9. Cycling 10. Wrestling

MURDER MOST FOUL

WHO KILLED THE FOLLOWING FAMOUS FIGURES?

1. Robert Kennedy

2. Billy the Kid

3. The Minotaur

4. Abraham Lincoln

5. Eddie Royle in EastEnders

6. Emperor Claudius

7. Wild Bill Hickock

8. Cock Robin

9. Shakespeare's King Duncan

10. Gianni Versace

ANSWERS
1. Sirhan Sirhan 2. Pat Garrett 3. Theseus 4. John Wilkes Booth 5. Nick Cotton
6. Agrippina – his wife 7. Jack McCall 8. The sparrow 9. Macbeth 10. Andrew Cunanan

STRIP TEASERS

IN WHICH NEWSPAPERS, COMICS OR MAGAZINES DO THE FOLLOWING CARTOON STRIPS APPEAR?

1. *Korky the Cat*

2. *Beau Peep*

3. *Dan Dare*

4. *George and Lynne*

5. *Fred Bassett*

6. *The Bash Street Kids*

7. *Roger Melly*

8. *The Perishers*

9. *Rupert the Bear*

10. *The Four Marys*

ANSWERS
1. *Dandy* 2. *The Daily Star* 3. *The Eagle* 4. *The Sun* 5. *The Daily Mail* 6. *Beano* 7. *Viz* 8. *The Daily Mirror* 9. *The Daily Express* 10. *Bunty*

OCCUPATIONAL HAZARDS

....

WHAT ARE THE OCCUPATIONS OF THE FOLLOWING TV CHARACTERS?

1. Harold Steptoe

2. Bernard Hedges

3. Trigger

4. Geraldine Grainger

5. Gladys Emmanuelle

6. Jacko, played by Karl Howman

7. Terry McCann

8. Niles Crane

9. Douglas Ross

10. Della Street

OLOGISTS

WHAT IS STUDIED BY THE FOLLOWING SPECIALISTS?

1. An ornithologist

2. A seismologist

3. A cosmologist

4. A cryptologist

5. An entomologist

6. A palaeontologist

7. A herpetologist

8. A toxicologist

9. A graphologist

10. An orologist

ANSWERS

1. Birds 2. Earthquakes 3. The Universe 4. Codes 5. Insects 6. Fossils 7. Reptiles 8. Poisons 9. Handwriting 10. Mountains

GRAMMYS

**NAME THE RECORDING ARTIST WHO
WON A GRAMMY FOR THESE ALBUMS OR SINGLES.**

1. The album 'The Joshua Tree'

2. The single 'Bette Davis Eyes'

3. The album 'Can't Slow Down'

4. The single 'Don't Worry Be Happy'

5. The album 'Graceland'

6. The single 'Wind Beneath My Wings'

7. The album 'Jagged Little Pill'

8. The single 'Tears In Heaven'

9. The album 'Faith'

10. The single 'All I Wanna Do'

ANSWERS

1. U2 2. Kim Carnes 3. Lionel Richie 4. Bobby McFerrin 5. Paul Simon 6. Bette Midler 7. Alanis Morissette 8. Eric Clapton 9. George Michael 10. Sheryl Crow

SAINTS ALIVE

WHO IS THEIR PATRON SAINT?

1. Dancers

2. Gardeners

3. England

4. Farmers

5. Tax collectors

6. Carpenters

7. Dentists

8. Athletes

9. Children

10. Brewers

ANSWERS

1. St Vitus 2. St Adam 3. St George 4. St Isidore 5. St Matthew 6. St Joseph
7. St Apollonia 8. St Sebastian 9. St Nicholas 10. St Wenceslaus

SINGERS ON CELLULOID

NAME THE FAMOUS POP STARS WHO STARRED IN THE FOLLOWING FILMS.

1. *Desperately Seeking Susan*

2. *The Delinquents*

3. *Summer Holiday*

4. *The Bodyguard*

5. *The Best Little Whorehouse In Texas*

6. *Caveman*

7. *Brimstone And Treacle*

8. *Silver Dream Racer*

9. *Mad Max Beyond Thunderdome*

10. *The Wedding Planner*

ANSWERS
1. Madonna 2. Kylie Minogue 3. Cliff Richard 4. Whitney Houston 5. Dolly Parton 6. Ringo Starr 7. Sting 8. David Essex 9. Tina Turner 10. Jennifer Lopez

SUPER HEROES

....

NAME THE SUPER HEROES FROM THEIR SECRET IDENTITIES.

1. Clark Kent

2. Diana Prince

3. Doctor Banner

4. Peter Parker

5. Billy Batson

6. Dick Grayson

7. John Reid

8. Mark Harris

9. Kathy Kane

10. Henry Penfold, the mild-mannered janitor

ANSWERS

1. Superman 2. Wonder Woman 3. The Incredible Hulk 4. Spiderman 5. Captain Marvel 6. Robin 7. The Lone Ranger 8. The Man from Atlantis 9. Batwoman 10. Hong Kong Phooey

81

BATTLE STATIONS

NAME THE BATTLE ...

1. That was fought in San Antonio in 1836.

2. In which Horatio Nelson died.

3. In which William III defeated James II in 1690.

4. Also known as Custer's Last Stand.

5. Fought on Senlac Hill.

6. In which tanks were first used.

7. In which Robert the Bruce defeated Edward II in 1314.

8. Also known as the Battle of Aboukir Bay.

9. That was the first major land battle of the Falklands War.

10. Of 1066 that shares its name with a football stadium.

ANSWERS
1. Alamo 2. Trafalgar 3. Boyne 4. Little Big Horn 5. Hastings 6. Somme 7. Bannockburn 8. Nile 9. Goose Green 10. Stamford Bridge

PUPPET POWER

WHAT SORT OF ANIMALS ARE THE FOLLOWING PUPPETS?

1. Kermit

2. Basil Brush

3. Nookie

4. Muffin

5. Orville

6. Cuddles

7. Sweep

8. Tingha and Tucker

9. Hartley in *Pipkins*

10. George in *Rainbow*

ANSWERS
1. Frog 2. Fox 3. Bear 4. Mule 5. Duck 6. Monkey 7. Dog 8. Koala bears 9. Hare 10. Hippo

WISH YOU WERE HERE

....

IN WHICH COUNTRIES ARE THE FOLLOWING HOLIDAY DESTINATIONS?

1. St Tropez

2. Copacabana Beach

3. Rimini

4. Buggiba

5. Hammamet

6. Colwyn Bay

7. Sun City

8. Luxor

9. Montego Bay

10. Nerja

ANSWERS
1. France 2. Brazil 3. Italy 4. Malta 5. Tunisia 6. Wales 7. South Africa 8. Egypt
9. Jamaica 10. Spain

WHAT THE DICKENS

....

NAME THE DICKENS NOVELS THAT FEATURED THE FOLLOWING CHARACTERS.

1. Sir Thomas Clubber and Augustus Snodgrass

2. Miss Havisham and Philip Pirrip

3. Jack Dawkins and Agnes Fleming

4. Uriah Heep and Clara Peggotty

5. Madeline Bray and Wackford Squeers

6. Sydney Carton and Charles Darnay

7. Jacob Marley and Mrs Fezziwig

8. Tom Jarndyce and Sir Arrogant Numskull

9. Doctor Jobling and Sarah Gamp

10. Thomas Gradgrind and Stephen Blackpool

ANSWERS
1. *The Pickwick Papers* 2. *Great Expectations* 3. *Oliver Twist* 4. *David Copperfield* 5. *Nicholas Nickleby* 6. *A Tale Of Two Cities* 7. *A Christmas Carol* 8. *Bleak House* 9. *Martin Chuzzlewit* 10. *Hard Times*

THE GOOD BOOK

WHICH BOOK OF THE BIBLE ...

1. Is the first of the Old Testament?

2. Is the first of the New Testament?

3. Is made up entirely of letters or correspondence?

4. Has the shortest name?

5. Shares its name with a Bob Marley album?

6. Other than 'Ruth' is named after a woman?

7. First lists the Ten Commandments?

8. Is the first alphabetically?

9. Is the last alphabetically?

10. Is the last book?

ANSWERS

1. Genesis 2. Gospel According to Matthew 3. Epistles 4. Job 5. Exodus 6. Esther 7. Deuteronomy 8. Acts 9. Zephaniah 10. Revelation

WORD LINKS

....

WHAT WORD CAN GO IN THE BRACKETS TO END OR START EACH PAIR OF WORDS?
E.G. WATCH (DOG) COLLAR.

1. French (   ) Shopping

2. Sun (   ) Cake

3. Clock (   ) Trick

4. Traffic (   ) Jar

5. George (   ) Baby

6. Rat (   ) Horse

7. Jail (   ) Down

8. Blood (   ) Hood

9. Chair (   ) Hole

10. Hair (   ) Work

VIVE LA FRANCE!

WHAT IS THE NAME OF ...

1. The French underground system?

2. France's annual film festival?

3. The oldest university in France?

4. The major champagne region in France?

5. A library in French?

6. The national flower of France?

7. The art gallery that houses the *Mona Lisa*?

8. The French national anthem?

9. The international French Rugby Union ground?

10. The last Emperor of France?

SHARED FILM ROLES

WHICH ROLE WAS SHARED BY EACH GROUP OF THREE ACTORS?

1. Douglas Fairbanks, Michael York, Gene Kelly

2. Alec Guinness, George C Scott, Ron Moody

3. Gary Oldman, Christopher Lee, Bela Lugosi

4. Charlton Heston, Mel Brooks, Burt Lancaster

5. Albert Finney, Tony Randall, Peter Ustinov

6. Richard Burton, Charles Laughton, Sid James

7. John Gielgud, Rex Harrison, Kenneth Williams

8. Sean Connery, Richard Harris, Anthony Hopkins

9. Peter Cushing, Peter Cook, Basil Rathbone

10. George Hamilton, Tyrone Power, Antonio Banderas

ANSWERS

1. D'Artagnan 2. Fagin 3. Dracula 4. Moses 5. Hercule Poirot 6. Henry VIII 7. Julius Caesar 8. Richard the Lionheart 9. Sherlock Holmes 10. Zorro

TV ANAGRAMS

UNRAVEL THE FOLLOWING ANAGRAMS TO GIVE THE NAME OF A TV PROGRAMME.

1. KART REST

2. STAR DIM MEN

3. TART GAG

4. SILLY BAKE SLANG

5. HIT BELL

6. KERB CAD LAD

7. CAIN RACED MAD

8. DEATH FRET

9. A SLAY CUT

10. RED ROSE OIL LIDS

ANSWERS

1. Star Trek 2. Mastermind 3. Taggart 4. Ballykissangel 5. The Bill 6. Black Adder 7. Candid Camera 8. Father Ted 9. Casualty 10. Soldier, Soldier

THEY DIED IN 2000

NAME THE FOLLOWING FAMOUS PEOPLE FROM THEIR INITIALS AND THEIR AGE WHEN THEY PASSED AWAY.

1. SM – aged 85, died in February

2. JG – aged 96, died in May

3. PY – aged 40, died in September

4. ID – aged 57, died in March

5. AG – aged 86, died in August

6. EM – aged 82, died in November

7. RD – aged 76, died in August

8. WM – aged 79, died in July

9. CK – aged 73, died in April

10. CS – aged 77, died in February

ANSWERS

1. Stanley Matthews 2. John Gielgud 3. Paula Yates 4. Ian Dury 5. Alec Guinness 6. Eric Morley 7. Robin Day 8. Walter Matthau 9. Charlie Kray 10. Charles Schulz

A TEST OF TRIBES

IN WHICH COUNTRY DO THE FOLLOWING TRIBES OR RACES OF PEOPLE ORIGINATE?

1. Maoris

2. Basques

3. Sherpas

4. Aztecs

5. Tamils

6. Picts

7. Aborigines

8. Gauls

9. Incas

10. Magyars

COVER TO COVER

NAME THE POP SONG THAT HAS BEEN RECORDED BY EACH GROUP OF THREE ARTISTS.

1. Showaddywaddy, Nick Berry, Buddy Holly

2. The Mindbenders, Phil Collins, Les Gray

3. Elvis Presley, UB40, the Stylistics

4. Tommy Steele, Guy Mitchell, Dave Edmunds

5. Big Fun, the Jacksons, Clock

6. Barry Manilow, Donna Summer, Take That

7. The Drifters, Bruce Willis, the Tom Tom Club

8. The Communards, Harold Melvin, Thelma Houston

9. David Bowie, Eddie Floyd, Aimi Stewart

10. Dusty Springfield, Samantha Fox, the Tourists

ANSWERS
1. 'Heartbeat' 2. 'A Groovy Kind Of Love' 3. 'Can't Help Falling In Love With You' 4. 'Singing The Blues' 5. 'Blame It On The Boogie' 6. 'Could It be Magic' 7. 'Under The Boardwalk' 8. 'Don't Leave Me This Way' 9. 'Knock On Wood' 10. 'I Only Want To Be With You'.

CAR TROUBLE

NAME THE CAR MANUFACTURERS THAT MADE THE FOLLOWING MODELS.

1. E Type

2. Quattro

3. Cherry

4. Xsara

5. Avenger

6. Interceptor

7. Cavalier

8. Edsel

9. Polo

10. Primera

ANSWERS
1. Jaguar 2. Audi 3. Datsun 4. Citroen 5. Hillman 6. Jensen 7. Vauxhall 8. Ford 9. Volkswagen 10. Nissan

THE FINAL WORD

REPUTEDLY WHOSE WERE THE FOLLOWING FAMOUS LAST WORDS?

1. 'Et tu Brute.'

2. 'Wait till I have finished my problem.'

3. 'I am just going outside and I may be some time.'

4. 'Get my swan costume ready.'

5. 'Let not poor Nellie starve.'

6. 'That was a great game of golf fellas.'

7. 'Let's do it.' (Just before his execution)

8. 'I shall hear in heaven.'

9. 'So little done, so much to do.'

10. 'That was the best ice cream soda I ever tasted.'

ANSWERS

1. Julius Caesar 2. Archimedes 3. Captain Oates 4. Anna Pavlova 5. Charles II 6. Bing Crosby 7. Gary Gilmore 8. Beethoven 9. Cecil Rhodes 10. Lou Costello